Maths QED CLUB

Adding and Subtracting Book 2

Ann Montague-Smith

25   37

QED Publishing

QED

Copyright © QED Publishing 2005

First published in the UK in 2005 by
QED Publishing
A Quarto Group company
226 City Road
London EC1V 2TT

www.qed-publishing.co.uk

A Catalogue record for this book is available from the British Library.

ISBN 1 84538 196 3

Written by Ann Montague-Smith
Designed and edited by The Complete Works
Illustrated by Peter Lawson
Photography by Steve Lumb

Publisher Steve Evans
Creative Director Louise Morley
Editorial Manager Jean Coppendale

Printed and bound in China

With thanks to:

Contents

Adding small numbers

Add each set of numbers on the cars. Find that total on a driver's helmet. That's the driver of that car!

1+2+3

4+2+5

5+3+2

3+4+2

11

13

10

What happens if you add the numbers in a different order? Is the total the same or different?

4+5+3

Use the numbers 1 to 10.
Find three numbers which make a
total of 20. Can you find 5 different
ways of doing this? Check your totals
by adding in a different order.

9+4+7=20

6+4+3

4+7+3

6   12   9   14

5

I know these

You will need a friend, a coin and two counters. Take turns to throw the coin onto the spinner. Move your counter forwards the number your coin lands on, and answer the question on the lily pad. If you answer correctly, leave your counter there. If you are wrong, move back to where you were. The winner is the first one to the finish.

Start

5+4

3+6

50+50

4+2

5+3

30+70

5+5

7–2

8–3

5–3

8–7

10–10

100–80

4+6

10+90

1 2 4 3

Now try this

Use three of these numbers:
1, 2, 3, 4, 5, 6, 7. You can only
choose each number once for each
addition sentence you come up with.
Write 4 different addition
sentences with the total of 10.

$3+6+1=10$

100–30

100–60

8+2

9+1

20+80

2+8

10–5

3+7

20+8

100–50

40+60

9–3

6–6

6+2

Finish

1+9

100–100

7

I know totals for 20

You will need 21 counters or coins. Choose two numbers from the animals that total 20. Cover your numbers with the counters.

Find different ways to make a total of 20. Can you cover 20 of the numbers?

Challenge

Look at the numbers on the animals. Add 2 numbers together to make a total of 30. Can you find 5 ways of doing this?

?+?=30

0
14
17
12
2
15
16
18
1
7
3
5
9

5 and a bit

You can break numbers up into '5 and a bit' to make adding easier like this: 9+7=5+4+5+2=10+4+2=10+6=16. Now you can work out how many bones are in the dogs' bags.

Try this with a friend

Take turns to choose two of these numbers: 31, 32, 33, 34, 35.

Write an addition sentence using your numbers. Write the answer.

Tell your friend how you worked out the answer.

$$35+31=30+5+30+1=60+5+1=66$$

You can break tens and units numbers up in the same way like this: 13+22=10+3+20+2=30+5=35. How many fish do the cats have in their bags?

14 25

16 13

17 27

18 21

Adding and subtracting

If you know an addition fact, then you can work out more facts like this: 16+3=19   3+16=19   19-16=3   19-3=16

16,3,19

15,8,7

18,11,7

4,19,15

20,4,16

11,5,6

Look at the numbers on the donkeys.
Find 4 different number sentences for each set of numbers.

Now try this

Look at these 6 numbers:
4, 15, 7, 3, 12, 11. They are mixed up.
Can you sort the numbers into
two sets of 3? Each set of numbers
must make 4 number sentences.

?+?=?
?+?=?
?−?=?
?−?=?

12,5,17

3,13,16

4,16,12

11,14,3

4,13,17

13

Tens and units

Help the postmen and postwomen work out how many letters to put into their bags by finding the answer to the number sentences on their post bags. An easy way to work this out is to add or subtract the tens first, then do the units.

92–51

31+47

67–13

23+41

48–15

Which bag will have the most letters in it?
Which bag will have the least number of letters in it?

64+23

43+36

76−23

85−62

44+32

54−24

Try this

Choose a number from here:
20, 30, 40, 50, 60.
Now choose a number from here:
15, 17, 23, 26, 38.
Add the two numbers together.
In the answer, what do you notice
about the tens and the units digits?
Try this 4 more times.

20+15=

Finding small differences

Find a butterfly with the same number difference as the orange one. Count up from the smaller to the larger number to find the difference.

Find the other pairs of butterflies with the same difference.

62 − 54

45 − 39

Challenge

Use two-digit numbers.
Find 5 pairs of numbers
with a difference of 6.
Write your pairs of numbers down.

64 − 58 = 6

81 − 78

61 − 57

73 − 67

51 − 46

Four in a row

You will need some counters. Choose 2 numbers from the animal statues below. Decide whether to add or find the difference between your numbers. If your answer is on the grid, cover that number with a counter. Try to make a line of 4 counters from your answers.

89   16

96

26

40   79

63

7

33

17

23   43

Play the game with a friend.
The first one to get 4 in a row wins!

Try this

Make your own 4 in a row game.
Write some numbers that can be added
or subtracted. Write the answers in
a grid. Write some more numbers until
the grid is full. Now ask your
friend to try to make 4 in a row.

72

36

9

10

53

13

69

49

56

19

Seaside shopping

You will need some coins. Pretend to buy 2 of the things below. Give the correct amount of money in change.

45

84

71

42

79

Now try this again. This time, give too much money when you pay. Work out the correct change.

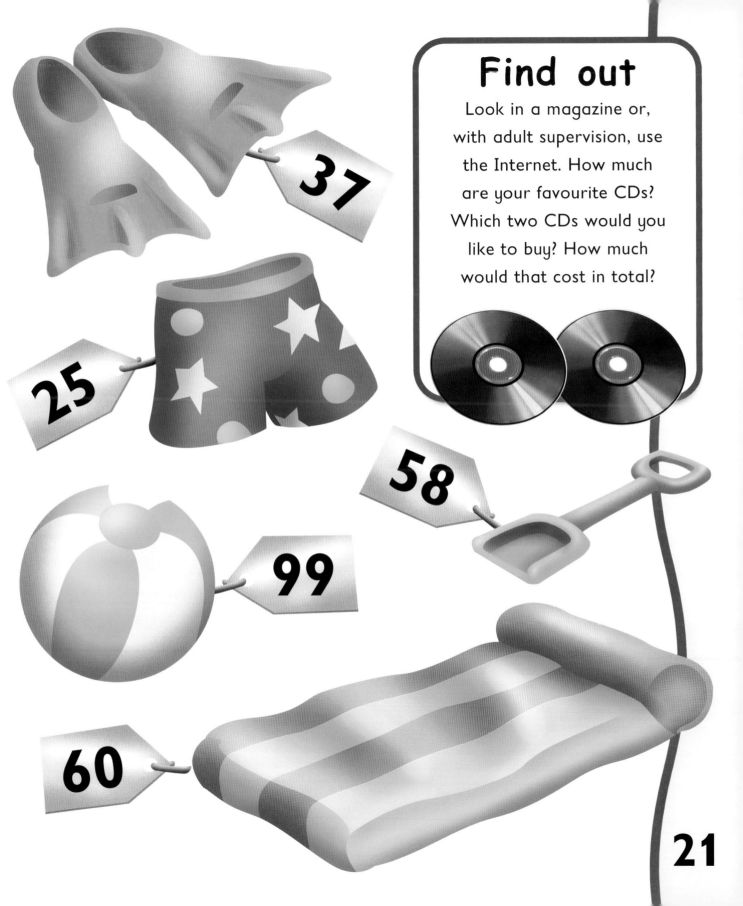

37

25

Find out

Look in a magazine or, with adult supervision, use the Internet. How much are your favourite CDs? Which two CDs would you like to buy? How much would that cost in total?

58

99

60

21

Supporting notes

Adding small numbers – pages 4–5

If the children need further help, there are two strategies that they might find useful: finding pairs of numbers which make 10, then adding on the third number, such as 4+7+6=4+6+7=10+7=17. Or, putting the largest number first, such as 3+5+4=5+4+3=9+3=12.

I know these – pages 6–7

Encourage the children to answer these questions as quickly as they can. These are addition and subtraction within a total of 10, and addition of decade numbers to 100. If children are unsure, remind them of strategies that they already know, such as counting on from the larger number, and using what they know about single-digit totals to 10 to find decade totals up to 100.

I know totals for 20 – pages 8–9

Knowing totals for 20 is an extension of knowing totals for 10. For example, 2+8=10 and 12+8=20. If children are unsure, cover over the teen digit and ask the children to total the units to make totals of 10, then uncover the teen digit to make a total of 20. Encourage the children to spot the pattern: 0+20=20; 1+19=20; 2+18=20…

5 and a bit – pages 10–11

Encourage the children to work mentally, where possible, when partitioning and recombining. If they are unsure of this, then encourage them to write addition sentences which show the partitioning and recombining of the numbers.

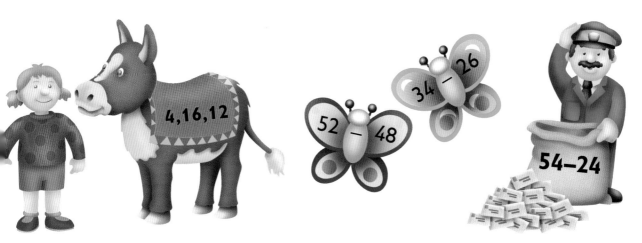

Adding and subtracting – pages 12–13

If the children know, or can rapidly recall, one addition or subtraction fact, then they can deduce three other facts. If children are unsure about this, write down one of the facts like this: 16+3=19. Then ask, 'What is 3+16? What do you notice? So what is 19-3? And 19-16? Now what do you notice?' If the children find the calculation difficult, count together using a mental number line.

Tens and units – pages 14–15

Where the addition or subtraction of the units does not cross the tens barrier, the children can use what they already know to work out the answer. They will probably find it easier to begin with the tens digits, then deal with the units. If they are unsure, use a number line and start with the tens digits.

Finding small differences – pages 16–17

Counting up from the smaller to the larger number is a useful strategy when finding small differences. If children are unsure, use a number line. Start at the smaller number and count up in ones. The children can keep track of how many are counted on their fingers. Encourage them to move to doing this mentally.

Four in a row – pages 18–19

This game challenges children to use addition or subtraction facts that they know, or can calculate mentally. They may find it helpful to have paper and pencil handy when playing this game, so that they can jot down which numbers they have tried and the totals or differences.

Seaside shopping – pages 20–21

Children will find it useful to have real coins for this activity. If they find the totalling difficult, they can begin with a selection of coins and count out what they need for each price, then total the coins. Encourage them to total mentally, then count out the coins, using the fewest coins possible.

Using this book

The illustrations in this book are bright, cheerful and colourful, and are designed to capture children's interest. Sit somewhere comfortable together as you look at the book. Children of this age will normally be able to read most of the instructional words. Help with the reading where necessary, so that all children can take part in the activities, regardless of how fluent they are at reading at this point in time.

The activities in the book include recall of addition and subtraction facts for all numbers to 10, such as 3+6; 9-1... The children use what they know about addition for a total of 10 to make totals of 100 using decade numbers, such as 60+40. They add and subtract tens and units, using mental methods. Encourage the children to use mental methods, such as counting up in ones to find small differences. For example, for 52-48, count up from 48 to 52: 49, 50, 51, 52. The children can keep a tally of how many they have counted on their fingers at first, and then move to doing this mentally. Where the children are combining tens and units, they may find it helpful to make some notes on paper. One way of working out, for example, 36+57, is this: 36+57=30+6+50+7=80+6+7=80+13=93.

Encourage the children to explain how they worked out the answers to the questions. Being able to explain their thinking, and to use the correct mathematical vocabulary, helps the children to clarify in their minds what they have just done. Also, where there are children who are not so sure of how to solve the problem, hearing what others did, and how they did it, helps them to use these methods more effectively.

Do encourage the children to make notes as they work at an activity. They can record numbers, writing them in order, or write simple sentences to explain. Encourage them to be systematic in the way that they work, so that they do not leave out a vital part of the evidence that they need to find a solution.

Above all, enjoy together the mathematical games, activities and challenges in this book!